Capitalism Calls Poetry Lazy

A strangely Whitmanic collection... the "I" is tormented, and the America is seemingly unworthy of love, now, but the Love is there in the poems and in the "I" -- who twists and changes (gay man/woman/witch/natural seer), amuses the reader, observes itself, the Southwest, the nation and its wars, knowing itself to be a detailed participant among objects and technology and jobs. This book is also a surprising, real history of the last, say 50 years. Beautiful, intelligent poetry.

–Alice Notley, award winning poet

Felt along the arm and into the stomach, Wyatt Welch writes poetry our bodies remember. A masterful poet who holds a lens from their life to connect the ramifications of our living. I will always keep this extraordinary book like an oracle and warning that knows, "If you're a wild creature, you'll be wiped away."

–CAConrad, author of *AMANDA PARADISE: Resurrect Extinct Vibration*

This book offers its readers equal parts delight, activation, and reverie. Each line is impeccably crafted, as is the balance Welch weaves between beauty and grief, love and offense, anger and aplomb. *Capitalism Calls Poetry Lazy* is a volume of gripping, exquisitely beautiful poetry that calls *out* humanity's atrocities while calling the reader *in* to a capaciousness that can hold it all.

–Roxy Runyan, author of *Poems for Crones*

CAPITALISM CALLS POETRY LAZY

FLOWERSONG
PRESS

poems by
Wyatt Welch

FLOWERSONG
PRESS

FlowerSong Press
Copyright © 2022 by Wyatt Welch
ISBN: 978-1-953447-58-6
Library of Congress Control Number: 2022938688

Published by FlowerSong Press
in the United States of America.
www.flowersongpress.com

Cover Design by Priscilla Celina Suarez
Set in Adobe Garamond Pro

NOTICE: SCHOOLS AND BUSINESSES

FlowerSong Press offers copies of this book at quantity discount with bulk
purchase for educational, business, or sales promotional use. For information,
please email the Publisher at info@flowersongpress.com.

Contents

Acknowledgments

I'd like to thank Roxy for the strength of her sisterhood.

Some of these poems or their earlier versions have appeared in the following publications: *Aired, Persephone's Daughters, the Mantra Review, deLuge Journal, Harpy Hybrid Review, the Ocotillo Review,* and *the Anacua Literary Arts Journal.*

CAPITALISM CALLS POETRY LAZY

The House a Glass Dark Beautiful

Rose-stained it the window night behind

        the light's moon so I want to know
where does it come from

      the soul, you, exist, you are, like

acting, you are, acting to make friends

        for what you need,

tho you are reading the words I'm thinking, Ramen noodles
you are the world across the room, laughing at coffee

the city I can't speak for, for city
is another's mind and we aren't the only

one's talking, why

does my heart   make decisions

     about you, but if
I am designed   to come from

where I have been. Still I
have one. Forgive me.

Tucson, 2017

I Can't Tell Time, 1980's

The on ramp's not finished yet go further down the road we'll hit
On another exit soon, this Shell station'll do
Bathroom mirror dingy greasy bar soap too dim, the
Discolored light stained-teeth light wall's grimy fine
All right I'll brush my teeth not here, use a water jug instead.

Park us near a light blue semi and try to sleep
Wave back at a cheerful yellow sun-dressed
Prostitute who waves first
Dad asks.

Gate in a field, February '85, Step-Mom disappears
We live in the stolen Budget Rent-A-Car
In '86, on white beaches, Cuban music, jalousie windows,
St. Petersburg, Florida I know the alphabet
Backwards and count in Spanish in that direction's
Palm Springs when we lived by a golf course.

We lived on interstate I-10 and 95 off and on during the 80's
All sorts of towns in Florida, small miserable towns is Upstate New York
I hate these towns the most, one stoplight and the rest's bars, I saw
At that age, Finger
Lakes Cattaraugus Indian
Reservation everything's in
Dad's white van, years later a beige Bronco but it was huger than a real Bronco
He called it "the Bear," and I'll mention the small red smashed truck
The crack in its windshield
Evokes a rightward-facing goose, son
Wild deer over there uh I see them now
He shoots them from the Bronco, a dark paradise of a rifle
We don't care whose farm this is
I see real snow for the first time.

In Franklinville or in Cuba or in
Wellsville or in Rochester or in Olean, New York

2

I don't speak much up here
I take the batteries out of some clocks
I say Eve isn't Adam's rib to the Yankee pastor, Pentecostals are what we'd
Call holy rollers and I done seen them talking in tongues
A kid pushes me into a shed
So I try to stab him with a fountain pen
I spent time breaking open
The November ice on Cuba Lake
I never go out far on any frozen lake, I'm afraid I'll break open
Up North I'm foreign and how ice works
Is new, is winter, isn't home.

Some afternoons
When the wind doesn't get too narrow on Cuba Lake
I think the jasmine and hibiscus back home in Florida, in Louisiana
Aren't all dead like they would be here, grow in the sunlight
Out of a future hollow sun
The light there makes it so different who are you?

Can I tell you
The 80's had more trains
More moments of roadside blackjack pine
A passing
Freightline they're
Wielded to haul
Southerners call them Poor Man's Carousels and a real hand waves back from
In the boxcars
Exploding by
I watch them
Hit a dog
And vanish
Under the wheels.   Keep it

To myself over the truckstop breakfast Mississippi, OK I
Speak like myself like an empty room don't be too loud
Hear the waitress say "Cold War," but you don't scare me
Russians don't scare me, see I don't blink, Dad where's Cuba? "It's close

So close, son,
They can swim

To our streets." For years I
Hold up US maps and sound out the place names
I love this map's sounds, my first real poems
Quartzsite, Opelousas, Ozona, Shenandoah
Kick a rock
In a river wow it's dry
Not a real river, but they call it one they're lazy, it's my
Third time living in California and there
Ain't no water here neither.

We moved from place to place after my dad
Kidnapped me from my mother in '79
If we move we have to really move, I come home from school and we'd leave
Without telling anyone
I was rarely in school for the 80's
I didn't know how to read time
From a round clock
Or to make a dollar from the change in my small hands
But were you
To take I-95 to Northbound 83 on the Baltimore
Beltway there's a left exit ramp
They been putting in tolls now for years here. You and the roadworkers
Can see the Potomac and wonder
Where like you it's heading.

I Asked Dad If There Were Viet Cong Witches

Birds are dying all over North America I make a margarita.
Three green water-crisis limes, California.
Future people with Valley accents on fire Lol starving, eating grubs.

And how should I be held accountable?
I'm in the classroom, teaching English.

When I will be dead as birds, I'll all be
elemental, talc & brook, and maybe my hair
in the Atlantic or a Denny's I'm at my altar,
my medicine of objects a blue shell
from Puerto Rico or this feather from I forget where.

My dad talks about two young girls he killed in Vietnam
at Denny's Sunday night coffee a bottle of pills
that only cost him a few dollars from the VA
heart pills, high blood pressure pills, blood thinners
cause his real blood would kill him.
I think his pills should go to the girls in Vietnam.

He says the first girl had a collapsible razor-box inside her.
When he pees at the medical base in Da Nang,
piss goes in three different directions he shot her
as she was running away her body   pro pelled   in to bam   boo
from the impact.
She was just dangling there, he said, a red puppet in the green jungle.
That image really makes him chuckle.

In war, they move you, like numbers across a checkbook.
Sometimes I have English students from Vietnam.

Afterward, fill my tank
89 unleaded $2.54 a gallon Iraq Circle K.
Our movie stars are losing their minds.
Loss of creatures, water, languages Merry Christmas.
I'm in an I-10 hotel Arizona.
Gideon Bible. Neon saguaro.
When I taught English in China, everyone was wearing bluejeans.

Inquisition:
"Did you pull your mind away from Him?"

Woman:
"Often—yes."

Until, he's hung
and symmetrical, then how many of us
trade in our Feminism. Whose shirt is this? Winona Rider's
stolen shirts.

The second woman he kills is more "accidental."
He mistakes the back of a fleeing mother holding her baby
for a male Viet Cong sympathizer.
The bullets go through them both. He never brings it up again.

Military training video of
Viet Cong getting blown
apart eyes blown
out, like wicks.

But,
I don't no
how to talk to this poem another school shooting, Townville, SC.

It guess I have a lot to say about You.

_____

The money around us makes us
hard to hear, animals in a forest fire.

Who should we look to, who is it?

I think it's Women, especially our dead ones.

Insight, Nevada

At the IKEA table covered in colored glass,
when I'm alone the house is psychological
feel realer walls behind it. Staring out sink window
oatmeal, wash empty the water displaced
fresh white house with handcrafted cabinets where
I teach myself to hate him my friend pays no rent
the motions you're adult and you're emotionless
lights are due at the end of the month.

I'm afraid it feels good to hurt you,
but that doesn't mean I don't, too.

I don't want to speak real here, maybe I should walk
around the house talking to myself leave
dinner on the piano to get cold
I want your hand on me don't touch me no one's here
coyotes blow through Reno or is that a baby crying? I
framed my glass my child
searching my mother's face
for the road I come from.

Someone else with your name, a strange man,
holds my body down in a toystore. Quiet.

I keep coming back to the poetry of you.
Now an editor tells me to write this so I'm
clearer, better, You, improving my words,
because I have to defend myself even here in poetry.

I don't like this poem, but I'm not sorry I was

bad for you. Who laid
the white hands of my poem down
and covered my mouth, with fear?

Where I Gather Under You Flowers

When I write out of my teddy bear, I'm this many.

Poem, am I no
one at

night or you, next to me, the injury
                    of us, changing the colors on blocks, crayons I am not good.
        of myself, I cut a deck of cards.

I exist no matter what you say over me.

Real   beauty
doesn't   care
for the   face
having   dwelt
in your   mouth
chest &   breath
tasted   lovers
crushing   grapes
thrown each   word
said like a   stone
cast into the   world.

Really where
the toy of the heart seems to
say want want want what a
selfish child inside
I wake next to, the tarot card.

The High Priestess, in her stillness

that part of English, the part that doesn't speak,

        but comes   out of flowers.

Because I don't know if I'm being myself or someone else.
Because it arrives from the High Priestess. Because here

where else should I speak? When here

in my throat, there is no light at all. The future
is a terrible place for light, and the bed dark gathers.

Tucson, 2018

Azaleas

Water potted plants, my presence with words.

I come from existence. I am inseparable from words.

How do you participate in our language, Faggot?

People like me are killed by governments.

Well,   *I suck dick like an angel,*   for example.

What do Your words speak from?   What Victors, what Go-Getters!

The slurs lain   at the flowers of your mouth.

Dear, Physiques

Your hands draft the dark

      of my head. ashore blue pillows
This odd act called poetry,

      my lawn grows late. I try, holding you
Jojobas, back you slide my tongue, and when

      that gets wearisome, we fuck hungry.
An old country, we walk our town,

      your hand rides. toward my shoulder (two men!), in public
Afraid to caress. arm, wrist they kill for this, egrets

      in the morning, I stand in the mirror editing my hair.

I Hurt Most Pulling Up My Shirt

s/he is the first thought,   if I don't

              see skin, see you, Covergirl.

these two pronouns   called I.   what's

between my legs,   might as well be
between my arms   like shoulders   forget

what I put on &   separate, into   sleeves,

into blouse,   into flag the sun

has photodegraded
of country.

     I wear breasts in language.

I am laying

     on a blanket in someone else's desert, I was

        the window of my body so open so look away.

Camo Hat at the Montezuma County Fairgrounds

Wise from pain

      my story, so what?

you don't say my girl was

shoved

downstairs, a

      trophy of roses

what I saw   the magic

when I disappear.

            A piano,

        an altar,

            where I

        becomes hands

      that wash

seeds, I sing *My Country, 'tis of Thee*

        I was given

a feminine structure

            to remember

      that love

        desires
      to be fragile

and held

together

      by trouble.

              I was

on the Cyclotron

      and the kids

whirred before

      me the questions

    I filled out

turned my pen

         to the left

     to face the assessment,

        the blanks

unanswered.

  I see myself in blanks, lines

typed   to fill in,   Four Corners Home & Garden Show

   your tall grass, oh… you'll never change

    I am wearing your jeans, I am reading our journals,

      I remember the clothes

   I wore that night, ashamed
        I wasn't happy.

Cortez, 2021

She Isn't a Boy, She's Just Wearing Blue

I dreamt a blue sun over us
dim dreamt scent of sulfur
moves my long beautiful hair if
I really had
they'd kill me, too.

Thunder,
        enormous & orchestral, god-boom, the

pianowood
pulls itself out of tune when it's
        June's cool evening airs in Tucson.

Science tells us Stars are mere flaming wads of fucking plasma, Lol.
No longer are they strange legends, nor longer our goliaths. Fuck you
for turning our Stars into gas giants.

Other Scientists say listen to Coltrane, the genius
is in its asymmetry, "it's just tensions & resolutions,"
in the desert friends in Paris
are talking about people they know who died in English.

   I laid the hours of my dark blue
hands on the glass in the door
        the light

               a

     randomness   throu
                      gh   out
         it.

All the bombs made until I no longer remember myself.
I don't recall having made all these enemies. I want to forget you, the way you don't care.
I am tired of this country asking me to vote and to grieve for it.
Dipping myself in milk, I bore myself, I lost my mother.

Dream of petals surrounding a sexual core.

And out there,
where it's not a dream
I tell you with a (face in blue shadow)
how I felt when he "overwhelmed" me
in heavy-rose light, or when
I got a refund
for the huge biology college textbook, what a Cesar salad
I made on 6th street,
hearing birds, thrown through sky,
the most obvious place to place an angel, you're right.

Between self a kitchen table
I have begun to be unpublished
this is just for myself,
so that I am honest:

You are everywhere in my poems;
under my words and their flowers
music when my hands are outside
and I am without hands but when I have returned to them once more.

Been living in a fragile, jaded trailer
it has no rooms, no locks to keep you out,
there's a pallet for you in the kitchen
but I was served without eating, and do not
want doctors telling me any longer how to live. All of those futile spaces
that became a part of us, our growth, a face on a ghost
is pointless but put there by love.

I just looked like a girl, spoken for.
Wasn't a boy, I just liked the color blue, the Poetry Officer said
I have to disappear so I can cooperate with all of you pigeons,
that I might join his Robert Frost Poetry Club of New fucking England.

But My She and My I
begin vibrantly broken together,
a real family, made singularly, could we even die?

A poem is like a crystal, its various aspects at once.
With a poem, I can scream, for a change, into someone else.

Xanax Stanzas

It was a really hot year don't much remember 2017, someone spells my name wrong
taking it down for a table, don't know the lovely W and y combo, Dad
you get liver cancer via Agent Orange "Orange
would drip down on the soldiers," he pantomimes wiping it off his brow,
says the foliage liquifies into a bright jade froth upon the jungle earth.

The US sprayed 11.2 million gallons of the agent in Vietnam after '65.
The Red Cross says up to 1 million people are severely deformed, disabled,
and have severe health problems 40 years later, 2018. The pictures I search
for the babies I see I close my eyes I turn away.

Dr. Bradley at the VA gives dad 4 months to live.
With his time left, he watches the History Channel,
which convinces him Aliens built the Pyramids.

Maybe the Aliens

      built Agent Orange and maybe they

      bombed Syria and warmed the Planet.

I practice telekinesis   moving garnets
across the table, witchhazel essence, theater tickets,
an orgasm, the Dollar Store. I'll read a predictably wise,
dull poem in a renowned magazine.
It's like when White people move into the barrio,
soon a community is replaced with lawyer's offices.
These poems waiting to stand trial.
No one takes a shit in the *Paris Review*.

It's 2018, this year, when Dad dies February.
Not from the cancer, but MRSA,
which is "everywhere now, in gyms and hospitals" his nurse says kinda laughing.

I'm there the hours the gradual suffocation
in incomplete lungs, held his eyes in mine, us looking into us,
looking out from a darkness, then his eyes
let go of mine, then his
were black wells traveling my face.

I'm cleaning out his apartment.
Turtle Wax, wrist watches, cans
and cans of carrots he bought after watching that
Prepper show on the Learning Channel,
a good blue cooler I keep, duct tape,
all the flashlights he collected, iodine
tablets, bullets for a .32, that paperback
on Iran-Contra, gauze, Louis L'Amour
books, he loved the Western genre.

The hardest part was throwing his favorite clothes into the dumpster.

Each, pastel shirt
and the gross darkness,   lying together.

When I sleep like my father,
to ease the TV shows
I'm in the important house
He was going to shoot
his brains out in,
but a plagiarized haiku
in bank pen, "Don't blow your head off"
was the final, 5-syllable line.

                                        Japanese haikus
                                        don't count syllables
                                        they count moras so
                                    haikus are never there.

The War on Drugs, (Which Ones?)
The War on Chemicals?, Biological Warfare?, the Discovery Channel,
Without money for cable? The voices in beauty?
Probably on Food Stamps. Have you fed the dog, baby?
I ate some turkey. I turnt on the oven and talked to it.
That night I dreamt of

the Octomom holding Agent Orange babies.

God,

why didn't you
show up to
our Gay
rights rally, &
never do
my liberal
coworkers either oh
of course you support
gay rights why
would your absence
assume otherwise
maybe something
was on Netflix
you know that show
where red flowers pour
out of Syrian's heads?

But does a girl
really die if she
has Jesus?, asks the NRA.

WHITE NOISE!!!!!!!!!!!!!!!!!!!!!!!!!!!!!!!!

Does she resurrect? If God
killed his Only Son,
then how many sons does a President get to kill?

The people You paid my father to kill
to ensure your investments
were buried in his life, "when our boys die, son,

they're shipped home cold and white," like

my skin is White,
white   as the color
                of money.

Rattlesnake, 2011

A poem is a lot smaller than I give credit.
Only does so much   when it's somebody

else's   I feel locked up. I'm   on   Jackson Avenue
in the   shallow house pine   board ceiling.   I, rattlesnake mask.

Not big enough was as big   as a family
could get and   still not big   enough one roof we couldn't

foresee the adult   hurt   a   toy,

games   of   collapse, earth filled   in the old fears,

the oldest child   doesn't

possess

black flapping sleepless god nightmares I have to back away
to be someone   else's   son   I'm not my father
I'm in   therapy   telling you   about

the houses,   the truck stops,   anonymous wall,
a child wishing for suicide, search backwards   with my money,

write the room   small with less   words.

Now write a   poem about   the   ground
and how it endures our dead.

Jackson Avenue Coyotes

3:15 3525 Jackson Ave house at night.
The landlord says his ex-wife is an amputee.
The joke is she keeps losing things it doesn't even
Make any sense I'm preparing gumbo for a fundraiser
Carlos is up for his bond hearing for illegally washing dishes
Under a deadman's Social Security number hominy & bell peppers
This is bullshit we don't got enough celery text Chris to get more
Bought a black & white print of an Apache Ga'an Dance by Duke Wassaja Sine
Arrows zigzag across their arms 4 gyrating bodies dancing the fire
Wielding crisscrossing boards I cut my index finger slightly along a steak
Knife taste my blood I'm blaming that bitch for stealing my good
Knife I got in Phoenix I don't really know if she took it yet but
Who can appreciate the feeling of letting things go I read a story about White kids in
Apache Junction caught a wild coyote in a shipping crate starved it
Just to see it starve & he shrugged his rich little shoulders hunger was our strongest bond
Unlike love's a set of conditions that I meet for you like it's worth
Driving me to the airport or there were strange voices woke me twice
From sleep I really hear two people talking in the living room
A woman's voice being earnest, the man was agreeing I
Sat up in bed and sensed a wide brim blue hat of sapphire,
And a dried out locust, on her head, feathers, the voices
Stop when I walk in, I realized the voices
Weren't coming from people or ghosts,
They were coming from the house.

Down from the livingroom floor's water-lily tile seems
Blissful on Jackson Avenue set back behind large arroyos
White ivory blinding roof repels sun, coyotes
Passing eventually eat the cats, Jezuit & Quixote,
Find Quixote's arm by the wash, and then we cried,
There is an endangered coatimundi living in the shipping crates of garbage in the
arroyo,
The coyotes hunt neighborhoods, eat all the cats, and move on,
Please save the heels of bread I feed the birds.

It was the last house I knew you in. I dreamt
The walls were eating the house. I started to lose things in the rooms.
1930's Washburn upright against the pine lumber partition later moved
By the front door how, where
A small blue floormat bought wholesale with an Afghan pink blanket are by an
Unplugged second-hand lamp later broken when Quixote jumps on the mantle
Stupid driveway rocks my cousin thought were beautiful in a grass basket
A shimmering purple vase when the sun's in it, it's really 4:38 p.m.

The furniture are in reality.
Cabinetmaking, awning, pinewood
Façade pressboard and that peculiar
                                        angle
Of bedroom to bathroom
Making my body appear
In three rooms at the same time in
The mirrors.

The mirrors haunt this house, too.
The houses want us inside them, at night
Observing us sleep, wondering
Why we dream and why we separate
Into bedrooms, into individuals
Reside at 827 East Adams St. now I pay this rent,
Poster, paintings, pictures, postcard from Barcelona, poem by Frank O'Hara

today, Washington

today Washington

flattens

Syria to a peace what's even

left I'm sure

rebar & bone

got   the poem or I say's storm

talking   to earth.

Some women   are built by fire,

that gender,   & led by color, those clothes,

whose bodies   were transformed

to salt   in the looking-back.

He keeps   shuffling bodies

across documents so they're impossible to find.

Tonight, a Military Darkness,

covers Tucson, these late hours

too loud for rest.

24

Cartographies, HIV

                                    Rainclouds,

come from California shallow ones, a feminist in my thirties
that's a lot of misfortune today, I want to be younger in this poem.

He buys a house with a hot tub, installs a

satellite TV

I kiss his face, kiss his

Do what I feel is right? Another time a little more   my voice
                                                              says Lauren's
                              so grown up in her black dress but the black
high-heel strap cuts   into her foot and it hurts
to walk stairs   she says.

For years I
didn't tell anyone or him.

One night that fear woke me from the other side of the house,

I seen it   "in the room" with us,
upright sitting   a mass on the white ottoman
my mind wild with seeing it: :dark laceration, presenceless
looking back.
                    The next day,

there's talk of going to Washington,
his mom has cancer bottom left lung
& her trachea in a place they can't operate.

II

You're positive:　　　　:I'
m negative

I stand up in midsentence when we fuck we no longer fuck, we're contemporary.

I am not where I speak, I'm
at the openings, I don't tell you
what future I really see us having　　　the future
is already　　　a memory,　　　so what will I mean by that?

I'm the upturned boards of a childhood house.

I'm five in the Florida house,

refused to leave it after we left, they left
I'm the yard picking white jasmines
talk to no one I don't
talk for a couple years colossal
tangerine tree check it for tarantulas build a fort
in sawgrass, "no
I'm the mommy here
play with stones they're babies boys
play with stones like these each
stone's a shape on the continuum every shape of stone
hurts every shape of　　a boy hurts, too."

I didn't know I would be
alone, telepathic

and venomous, shapeless, on monitor: *pink grapefruit on a nightstand.*

Your friend Emily doesn't drink cocktails in her cocktail dress.

Our baby,
our extraordinary child,

　　　　"You,　look distant,"

Is some kind of apology? Where do you think I'm sleeping?

"I want to be a good person." I say, speaking language.

"I'm afraid I'll still love you when you're dying."

III

HIV,

is our future, is our when.

When is your eyes
confessions and ending
where you turned to look me in the

     distance,

          red spectrum, blood of yes,   that's what I mean.

Do you like roses? You do. My favorite is tiger lilies, and you remembered, I turn

               to hold you   like glass.

I dress nice our last night.

Eviction, Phone Lines On

1.

fingers on wood, pushing
skin wanting cocoon,

silk & phantoms, keep quiet.

2.

rhyme & hammer, each
vowel, victory

squished blueberry, palm blued,

raised arrow, to deer.

3.

A man tries to bury a forest child, rearranging
the paint on the house,

behind the bedroom door, disembodied

terrify colors on the wall
numb though

the future woman the future hall has
burned holes

into her forearms, find girl,
the yellow closet door

a body you now possess,
a dark, uncontrollable house

fence dripping from faucets
blackness pooling in the mugs

Does she kill spiders? a woman, now that history
floats beyond me.

4.

I'm full

of individuals, we

the children, we
are now the women, we

sinful the women, we
awake threatened,

sexual & disobedient.

Cassiopeia, Oregon

I came there,   to be,

among the witches,   automatically,

came to be,   transformed,   and taken,

among the witches,   thought I'd,

project myself, amongst dim amethyst,

Siskiyou pines,   I was,

two places,

in illusion & engine,

of the price,   in my head,

the first time,   I was real,

I took water,   out of the dream,

in the dream,   I'll know I don't,

want to leave,   why's that,

your name,   means,

someone,   expecting fire

II

I was,   underground myself,

where I have,   a permanent voice,   in the dark,

now write a poem,   with my heart,

locked inside it,   the first time,   I see your want,

is under,   a broken wind chime,

What do I,   look like?,

I feel,   handsome,   the mirror of you,

you call, my eyes,   slate,   the engine,

of the poem's,

    turning,

between lips,

    my body,

becomes one of your,   wild altars

III

The pines pull,   their sleep,

exist,   no matter,

push into,   my back,   pick,

up a hairbrush,   dip it in,   red ink,

around the others, my clothes,

      are homeless,

      the,   freedom of together

IV

How should I go about,   spreading your names,
across the floor,   of my poems?,

Behind, the garden-house window,

we fog,   the glass,   and the forest,

is gone

V

What I love for you,

hold it,   across,   our wild continent,

the red face,   of a wild dog,

hungry in the American,   barren,

beautiful Southwest,   light

We, the Marys

You'll have to do this alone, especially when you're alone
                        and there are so many of us

        in the ground, so you have to be flowers.

                You'll have to bury the children
they taught you to want, press
                their little faces into darkness.

Everyone just seemed like a cop. On TV burning Black churches, no invasion
of a foreign soil will free you,   so give yourselves persimmons

some of you will kill yourself—so you're standing in a red light?, some of you devoured

        by their windswept god, everyone
                                so very proud
you do this alone,
        in a self made false by bucolic expectations,   disobedient mushroom you are

        leaving your hometown for good, you learned when to leave the room,
hugging the cruelty inside your mother the mute   air of your fathers
                during the elemental years

                                I'm in   little shoes I see
                                    damage   performed in my father's eyes

but all the lovers, I wouldn't trade
        I taste you
        indispensable fruit,
                you are

        pouring water over a sword I am in love

                with our possibilities I stand on your field

35

holding kinder hands than arms, my breasts dreaming in my chest.

I demonized a conversation, but you listened from the palisades.

If I
were someone, even
        a stranger

        would you climb down from your weapons? Would you
        listen from their blades?

in difficult times,

after the Election of Trump

now you wait for something else
it leans in, on yourself
heaven against forehead, rain against cloud head
for the sea, in difficult times
leave the lights on   dead-bolt
portraits online, don't touch me please
touch me, lull, nearing me, and between this.

In difficult times, the stars
        aren't old they're far but the headlines
are nearer, are close enough
    though the event already happened and you're just now
    reading   its old light.

In difficult times,
        I'm always sad when I buy a weapon
this time a switchblade because each time a man
makes love to me at the gamble
of who finds out.

In difficult times, I went to the polls
even when I couldn't afford to
and bubbled in the monkey
who swore to take its terrorism elsewhere I'm sorry.

In difficult times, I am the City,
whom we speak for in
poems,   separate and I,   in our city,
our dream of   city,   who would
want to be   mentioned or known
by a country, no   We the City,   leave
the United States to poetry,   in poetry   the language
of less than our words.

37

In difficult times, my office was burning
the window   in sky the whiteness   are you stronger
than an office?,   but neither are you,   they have
my body filmed   but I was   not on fire, those Towers
in New York sky   for you to visit   I'm falling I'm
moving colors, in your air,   nor have, nor
may I never   understand it   and nothing other.

In difficult times, the extinction
of Great Animals   to our suburbs,
alphabetized in DNA banks,   this devastation
distilled down to a meme I click Like on Facebook.

In difficult times, in night
      slip off, leave empty
casings dreaming
never   kissing emptiness
but in language,   emptiness is named,
      so here we are,   more or less in love.

In difficult times, this isn't a poem—
because you're searching for something
greater than yourself, and I am not you.

When You Say, "I Don't Understand Your Poetry"

Afternoon azure heat, cashmere clouds, unconditional weather
medicine cabinet mirror,

    I'm looking into all the mirrors in the house

to see if they're working
the body I see tho I hardly know changing   my   life

the universe gave me a face it'll take

    it away awful happiness you depend

on beauty you don't know how to read poetry
tho down at the North Jetties

we tried to swim to Snake Island
against the current a room I close   my   teeth
in if there's just me in loneliness then I

am alone to write pictures
    still difficult to look at my life in them

don't think much of myself if
a window is like air moving through it

decompose   words to   make them

    push.

Later I'm painted five oval pictures (fuck you), whitish hue
who speaks first, doesn't matter, all the people

might as well speak, say some
    thing real here, I was sad every time

    you held my hand,

held dark diamonds, the black bouncing back
                I want You   drone   camera   light.

Junky Mitsubishi lots of rock in the floormat, glass shattered diamonds,
stripped wires, plastic dash,

       "I don't   understand the car. Why is this Mitsubishi

just sitting here?"
Tucson apartment complexes, red

crayon flowers,   your duplex wall.

       She's the empty lot,

I could say "people" are "empty lots" but
instead write how it feels
when looking at someone empty

       let the wind blow   away my photographs.

When the hour has long left and night's true cooler airs
              chill my bed,

chill hillsides, chill the Exxon Valdez,

         & the darkness is therapy, what isn't

poetry, vulnerability

the parking lot, the lot of love, apartment love,

       wanting the human to build off of   I know you're reading

with me to know this place could be in someone else.

       Tonight I'll dream I'm on fire,
              a woman who rides a bull.

Poetry Class

At the bro house a glass bottle shatters
a man yells losing his IPA
cleans up the glass with a mop whoop-di-fucking-doo
lights cigarette the woman young in a purple pull-over sits
shakes head Yes with a new sparkling man in red bandana Happy Thanksgiving.

You all are so terrible I think having a positive attitude is immoral.

No, I don't fucking want to
talk to myself, let alone You. Why bother the Poems.

You & I disappear into a white forgotten costume.

Failing myself, oh everyone's failing.
The poetry teacher said my poem was "didactic." What an asshole's word.
What does *didactic* even mean?

Oh, is that BORING? Well you're boring.

"Giving moral lessons as an ulterior motive."

We are so dishonest I have to dig the poems out of me,
and I still question them. "Are you a little ego puzzle?"

Nature is moral until my cat is the most moral thing I know.
My thought doesn't even talk when I say that.
"Fantasize about
beating myself up
into blues and whites and write
about that: the Police burning a piano."

Someone's over buying drugs. No fronting anyone,
that's the first rule of selling. There's a quartz crystal
shaped like a pill on my Bose speaker.

There's agate, chalcedony, tiger's eye, obsidian, a wooden frog,
a white salt-shaker fox and a blue-pepper shaker owl
tchotchkes, Is it didactic to say *tchotchkes* is a Yiddish word?
What's "Fuck you" in Yiddish?

Talk about objects. A few colors and sizes to anchor you
in my experience. Well, why would you?
Looking through my windows. You voyeur. You peeping Thom.
Nosey ass audience. Do I think I'm better than you?
Goddamn right I do, You Fucking Nazi.

I'm owed a better nemesis and I want my money back.

Am I wearing poetry now? Is my leg through the armhole? A poem starts
at the top of the page,   in that window,
got it up there on their prison wall.

There are strange settlements on BLM land in Nevada I could stay on,
become as weird as I can, a shitty millennial hippie
in the Sierra Nevadas I've never seen writing this from a black chair.
How beautiful that *Nevada* is Spanish for "snowy."

A thin, white cat napping on a microwave.
Fidel Castro dies today in a cinematic, Orwellian article!!

Hi, Facebook Friend!
You unfollow me; I unfollow you.
Unfollow each other
until we're clicking on mirrors.

Getting myself off, like some kind of little god.

A babydoll. Play with me. Touch me here or there. Wherever feels like fun.
Disgusting babydoll. Throw it in the rag bin. Pluck a button-eye red bloody out.
I peed on my
angel pillow
in Grandma's bed
wondered if I was
possessed by the Devil.
What was going
on in that apartment?

The Exorcist
was on TV. I miss
my Grandmother watching
the nightly news
with Tom Brokaw
or Dan Rather,
those heavy
handsome serious
men of 80's
journalism. Dan Rather
was born on Halloween.
I'm in the blue kitchen listening to Dvořák.

I am speaking from a musical place in myself, a black open flower.

I want to write to Witches. Fuck the rest of You.
        P.S., the coral reefs are white as bone.

I could start making bombs. Obviously, that would be ethical given the context.
Some hippie on the BLM says some all-loving nonsense, but I've
seen a meme saying, "Love is a human-shield" and the people in it smiling.

Give the cat water and the Mojave asters some.
That brown, sunning lizard doing push-ups. Memory of Florida kids
down the street shooting lizards with BB guns.

Days later I visit Roxy at work at the café, a young guy there just discovered Ursula LeGuin's

future novels of women and tells me about them like I wasn't 20 once.

I say "It's less about the future of women

        than it is their history. A relegation to the

supposed science-fiction category." Men deny us

anything I want my hands on Ben's lips on my palms.

Lana del Rey's song West Coast loops in livingroom.

Come in from out of early dream this morning in the dream in Florida jungle-gym
futuristic buildings of silver blue and white steel children were spilling out

of a donut-shaped structure for recess, there were no particular women but there were people behind the bulbous Epcot glass so it wasn't a LeGuinian future because I'm a real adult at 37 love is haunted.

We all should contemplate killing ourselves.
It is an important part of living, I tell her, the school counselor,
I'll tell her she did nothing for me, you just can't
for I if Existence, the Poem, is just where we edit look at me.

My Mouth Lonely of You

Though looking into wind and sometimes mesas, I get there.
Running hot water over dishes in Utah
with Ben near Bear's Ears I'm over here in my poem
being apart with myself, winning land
in the Cherokee Land Lottery, my ancestors move to Georgia.

You say things like Rwanda or Palestine in a room of Whites with money.
All employees must wash hands before returning to work.

Poetry is a real place, a candle
spill salt across white on a dark floor, then say the sea is blue
because it looks as wide as blue,
or should I be language.

When I was rinsing dishes among the mesas, I was born in Florida, 1979.
To be the kind of woman I must be, a man. Put the toilet seat down.

The large window, you could clean it with Agent Orange, my daddy says.
He wants to go back to Nam so I'm thinking him there; Jerry Crutcher's
blown open legs, and that other guy who stood up
to admire how beautiful falling flares were's head exploded.

Pull Me,
down into my head, Pull Me,
down until You have never spoken,
where I must speak, like light, and think
like a temperature, a house
surrounds a ghost.

I pledge this, and to me of darkness healed.

People are the only evidence we have of existence.
You have held, not held, in tears my hand.
I can't believe walking down the sidewalk our eyes alone.
I can't believe loss is human.

I,

of my head, NO!
MY HEAD IS FUCKING YOURS! and I will always hate you to my soul for that.

If You   kill Me   You can't   so you haven't

ever killed me   until You   comprehend what   You've done.

Ridiculous protest, walking down the street, "Love trumps Hate."
Love doesn't matter to people with money—and not even You believes in it.

Well, someone has to clothe myself I'm standing
in a navy denim jacket asking to click Your link:

a TV show, where they're fighting on an island
to turn it into a toilet.

I eat food with my head.

Eating of one's own Devil: Capitalism.

––––––––––––––––––

I know why You want the Internet on: You're married.

          It's raining in my desert,   against our houses and our windows,
          against our stupid cactus, against You:

The Pyramid builders.
The Colonists. The Tenants. Their Broken Lease.

The political, occult parties, their Masonic symbols,

"He moved his hands up my Basilicas."

And their hero stories are all about grabbing ass:
Gilgamesh or Gilligan or Gillian from the X-Files
and the long, American boys of the United States of Vietnam.

Tonight,
my mouth is lonely of you.

I dry myself
off with stolen Marriott towels I don't care
if you hate my poems anymore.

New Microsoft Word Document

Descend. Stoop into

     down & between go
into moths. Down among

     thousands of quaking

black dark sparks. De-

com-   pose until

     moth   becomes

     a place. Life's darkness around me the tunnels.

          down in poetry, you push
       against someone
       else's barrier. If we were to

fall like tunnels
or the wind   of a blast

Though I have a poetry,
what have I

said with it, asks the moth-structure, speak with
          iodine in your thyroid,

and fire in your night.

There is something below us that doesn't need language;
         there are many women now writing poetry.

In our time we are but thinking the city. Taking OxyContins and Border Patrol Agents
to our beds. He says I must sign in:

dub dub dub dot
blah blah blah dot com.

They're taking children into His Office.
To be registered. In the Office,
I don't know who I am, am under whose authority,
an 8-year-old boy dies on Christmas Eve,
in the Office nothing happens.

The Death in us uses us
to bloom Itself forward, turning us   into hours & minutes, fabric black orchids.

We'll never agree. I witness you all going to McDonald's. I can say that.
Stand in line but you don't order.
The employees are looking into light.

A soul's building,

our
Eyes speak

up in it.   I am a Witch: the Eve who reaches

for a snake to eat.
You instructed us,

and turned our world   into composite leaves, Carnivora, igneous,
                stratocumulus I hate this computer its air
        the pedals of money,   the oil,

                the diamonds, you're grinding.

I'm wise when I don't matter. I'm American, but that isn't real.
Someone with nice eyes very close to me keeps where I am from in a secret.
The shorelines and hospitals, blue storm

Not one acre is free: the militaries have taken everything.

I know stories that aren't real. The Flood. The Garden.
and no one seems to mind.
I'm pulling darknesses over my hands, moths.

The dark of
                salt & water, think with
          their awareness,
but I
                am not as the stars which have no heart I check my phone.

          You challenge
                power structures to be
          without them, Black Lives Matter.

I'm drinking from a thick grey plastic bag destined for the ocean.
Dad, Print your name
for the doctor, for your chemo.
They're taking my father's blood away, to clean it.
To clean the Vietnam from it.
"We had to." dad says.

Lie still   in moths and arch   my arms.

A curse
on your ludicrous and impossible Gods, enraged bleeding flames of brass faces,
puerile stick-figures, crayons in hand. Who gets to be in the room?

And they eat   my soul?, you say that, if I kiss your son.
You, the People, force your children to breed more children. You, the Society, your Gender is
          no one
                hiding between bodies.

What am I to a World Or its Swastikas?

This pain is not mine.   It belongs to me.

I want you to kill each other so that you would exist. I want you to speak me open at the light.

In the wind, without most like soul, you correct me, it's a tributary,
                                 we're drinking poisoned water.
                                 I don't want the Internet
getting into my poems, Vanna White. Despite how beautiful
a swastika may be, I'd like to buy a vowel, wait but You
may have never existed. You who gives

my date of birth to the Geico Lizard, I am shitting
in a public restroom a fan of zombie shows.

You and I in nothing like language
where
                    you listen with *your* words. I'm stuck
in small white blurred lights they're colorful.
Who's in the dictionary. Who's allowed into the room?

        God is   a little stanza, a little George Costanza

        a light that doesn't shine on us. Needs my laughter.
        To become ash ashes that are still, are beautiful. Still,

I think lovely, lance of light

on ocean, piece of light on breakfast. I can blow the wind out the back of my head
with a gun. You, who are
consumed by the public meme. He, who turnt
our World into shitty Subway sandwiches. Are we
remembering the city? I remember the glass breaking.

The 9/11 glass in that Big Apple Sky.

I am the human color White. I am white tree rune, Ehwaz. I am in the nursing
home I love you. I am a New Microsoft Word Document. I am wiping down
the fridge. I am the buzz of its light. I am nothing to say. I am dying across
the earth. I am eating dogs. I am who I was in love. I am a poem you called
unproductive. I am atomic, of coastlines, of vitamins. I am imagined and
fictional to myself. I am speaking with debit cards. I am made of pieces older
than speaking. I am a shadow of Washington. I am a contestant on Wheel of
Fortune deepthroating hotdogs.

Tucson, 2018

The District Tavern & Xena Ellison

Try and write in a space history hasn't, a poem works
with some camaraderie between

opinion & poet,   "Your sexism
                                              is mutual and true of heart.
                              What a blanket on leather yellow furniture."

                              "… be your crotch when you awake."

                                              A poem with sexism's presence,
            The woman eating potato skins wants to ask her date her boyfriend her husband if
the copper locket on the long chain in her breasts he gave her
      was hard to find or if
      it reminded him of her or where he got it, but she knows
            he'll make some comment about how great it looks between her tits or he'll go on
                        about how copper is mined in Utah and how it's needed
            for biological function and when the Romans used it for spears and cannons. She thinks,

he kind of looks like David Copperfield.

I'm wanting not to
write me in this straight-bar, like any bar,
or should I say hey men, I grow a beard for safety,

which feels like I'm two mirrors aimed into one another in a time of war.

When did I
stop writing like a man? I'm driving telling a dick joke going 80.

Not so, sissy, even if,
your voice *is* your poem
                  use a prissy voice, lisp, queen, woof.

"Gay" feels like "the deepest sensation

                                        of disappearance."   Yeah, Gay is
I no longer have a subservient mind, but my ass?   The poetry
is in my ass: You murderous fuckers put it there.

                If you find a word without a history, the men
will tell you how to spell it. All night,
                                I'm around men, real men, and so
                                aim to blend in. This poem
wants to blend, be of
                the space it represents, as I am its representation, I, too, sit, in stool.

You men keeping saying "Oh, it's not that bad, Matthew Shepard."

An iced vodka Redbull and a guy
                against
        jukebox leans a swastika

on his right arm placed seriously over Snow White and the 7 Dwarves—
"They all wanna turn!" an uncle of mine once said.

                I really hate the way you men talk, a lip-synching girl.

If you're born the wrong kind of girl,
a friend may post about you:

        Hey, all. We are
        asking for help
        in finding
        our friend, Xena Ellison. She
        was last

        seen at 1:45am Thursday
        morning leaving
        her house in the 7th ward

        wearing black fishnet
        shirt army fatigue
        booty shorts and black
        & white sneakers. She has waist
        -length box braids. We just want

to make sure she is safe & will
begin to look for her

body.   My body

this   booby-trap against me, again still me
I've lost, I'll wear
a cool dress I like,
and you kill for

it, a dress.

I lost the woman I am. I lost my soul untaught, terrible.

I lost my eyes become possible.

And so, I let my real eyes be disabused by discovering the pearl
of the sexist, living world.

Sandy Hook

The weather above us; us under buildings.
News of a school shooting and maybe a storm, the drizzle's

Tchaikovsky on the rooves,
our booze tho here, & lightning twice more
haphazard yard secondhand couch I love that a cloud

is just a cloud any direction I see it go.

"Hey, need anything from the store?"

"Yeah, we're outta milk."

NRA

Shot children began trending that year.
The spectacle generated millions in advertising.

And each time the money dripped from your chops,
you said God was watching us.

Look at all these ground-breaking potato chips!

Oh, a glass of milk so human
you could say it's property.

The national soul throws a football.
Throws drones up like confetti.

A very slowly never seen blue Southern sky so dark my gun.

Albuquerque Republican Headquarters

Not the same house, though different darks and my arms

                                      were made weak.

He ran   his oars   through me, held   my back,
screamed at me,
because he   likes something,

                 well anyone likes something
living in a 1st World Power, "you expect your armies
                                 to just fucking take it."

I am   a poem
standing like   a person
held   by a force,
words like   billboards.

I vote   to let wind sweep
in on lake light   willow leaning
my lover, agree and   subtle speak
a president does   and so doesn't
I rose up sexually
I vote for   who I would be
without our   asshole pillow commercials,
Men vandalizing
mass movements, I vote
to not brace for your
exhausting impact
it's one system
it's not listening, and what
journalism in the   clutter of one other
good would it do,   your mouth
around my ear, a lamp on in the ashes

whenever I look at our warfare,
at the depth of our goblet,   gilded, how long does it pour?
you have not my allegiance, (What named myself in pieces at night,) I
am a tourist, but you   memorized my face, opened prisons
like they were goddamn Christmas presents, soldiers don't assure   freedom of speech, we do
burning gameshows   Ferguson, Missouri
burning off these worthless ballots I choose
to no longer believe you, I was in elementary school
wouldn't put my hand over my heart   would not pledge
my allegiance to you   kill the home team   NASA shoots people
into space when they exploded the flames we all saw it from the school yard.

Rittenhouse

                                    Funny medical card funny cause
I didn't promise anyone organs
                        leave them in my past we never
loved the dead so much
                            enough to write but we love what we remember
wash clothes & my orange dishes yes home
                                    is a story I remember the news story
today, walks free, free as bricks yes bricks are heavy talk to us
address us, from your altar,   our common foundation, as if
we were a nation.

Demerols

When your death
returns you to earth
      then you
will be stood upon,
like a color
      you will be
buried like a pet or a stone
so while you
      count your pills
before you take them
red ones from blue ones,
      blue ones from white ones
where else
do colors go
      if not
inside the living?

Jeremy's 40th Birthday Party, Puerto Peñasco, Mexico

Deep off roadside alders, amber, a radio
melody, a sole split-
open broken coyote, green plop of jojoba roadside
trash, ocotillo, cattle fence, there's wind
whatever humanness I say they have's just poetry, subject
a boy in a river catching fish, desirelessness
is the desert's greatest operatic track in the car.

I'm most myself when I'm driving on the Interstates,
learn my other names, some empty, a lot of bowls
but this auburn sky, what translations are the body, dreamcatchers
in a gas station, cool, I have money for a Sprite,
we've stopped in Why, Arizona, Tohono O'odham Nation for fuel,
the wording on a Lay's potatochip bag that's beautiful eat
an ice cream bar Led Zeppelin, surely
I'm Satanic, blessed & fallow, a Witch,
I dreamt of that hole, you say's "goodness," weep, I weep for?
Excavating womyn from a rock.

I was born in the desert each time.
An earliest dark head, sodomy, thinking it's a
Man, accuses other things of being
Women, making a kind of economics
between my legs, price for oneself, your heart, a low goal
for the huge human being, a soul says
let the strange, blowing world turn in the arms
of a dark mind, how a crystal
mangles its own light, what a little engine
of jumbled light and Sun. I love you, Son.

Sonoyta, Mexico Federal Highway 8 touristy red
donkey party piñatas grey cinderblock buildings
I desirous to push against this car's walls
this poem's walls to push bed

against his walls of me
inside my walls
of the bed there's a woman
lipsticking the edges of her penis
I can't change that turn around
in my body a city
I keep visiting.

Slow cows, one wren
yawning on saguaro cold dull wind
thru passenger-side window car's going, a boy
small in the street waves Hi itches his neck I don't
wave back to be cruel, the rejection
in his handsome eyes, Rocky Point
and our white money for these Mickey Mouse mansions along the Sea of Cortez
the first night I'll dream the phony houses are cardboard ghostships
adrift, backlit along the ocean, bobbing stupidly,
Cortez is here landing ashore declaring my dream his
no real edge at all it's happening to me,
here, from who I am real.

If I come with poetry to your birthday party
I can be somewhere else, or no one,
I'm always here, around straight people I didn't become
because in this poetry
you need me to trust that you're good, though good
is an American guy at your birthday party who says the word "future"
with that McDonald's confidence I hate.

"Progress shall put toilets under every 3rd World Ass,"
later he makes fun of fat people, plump fucking
slothful Mississippi people is his joke,
I say, "All bodies are beautiful," (say that to no one really, the air,
let it fall across myself), he's accepting of gay people enough
to hate fat people, typical
later I really laugh with everyone around cake & drink to puke
on wine and moonshine together Jeremy
checks in on me I'm humiliated by the brown vomit.
He cleans this up, this rare kindness
from a man moves me to silence.

I didn't mean to yield. We are all
so fooled by friendships, fooled in their agreements
and by one's own thinness the ocean tonight
sounds like the hallway around me the distance, but rather I
was called "incendiary" and "sensitive," a faggy porcelain doll
to burn, like a witch, who is just a word, I can say that
in English, in Mexico, why not, the Cortez shoreside
is a uniform black yet clad in the night's wind.

Where we come from,
over there, seeing the need for water in one another,
in other living things, or just each other, sometimes
I know you have moved on, but where did you move from?
How do you ever move at all, in the make-believe of Earth?

Radio Tucson

Doing key bumps at Eegee's
cause there's no
mirrors in Heaven spraypainted
Superman has the word *cunt*
on his forehead & a machete
thru Trump's head *fuck*
you puto over
his eyes a tweaker
steals a dreamcatcher
in a 4th Ave souvenir shop
hawking talavera
tchotchkes & Yaqui
baskets, mesquite
pod earrings.

Once again,
the summer night
gemshow oogles one
of them the daughter
who looks up
her glass eye &
that slumlord on 3rd
who manages
your shit-ass apartment
I move next to
a year from now
when I quit
my job peddling English.

Face
a hipster
with an under-bite
tending bar at Congress
her bumpersticker butt
hangs out, "What'll
it be" boot-
legged tattoos

down to
the small
of her back
in vendettas, some in
Hebrew, securing the front
register
with some apology.

You
toss me some
wit: Tucson's
on the negative
end of an underground
energyaxis
running from
Sedona Sedona's
on the positive
end it's
why here we don
black tees,
apocalypse It-Bitch
metal rings,
amethyst anklets,
another desertwelcomed
autumn
radioing birds
& anarchists in
from Portland,
New Orleans.

Maybe it was the feathery blur
dividing us birds to fly apart and so you entered.

You, Roxy,
now so present
in the burden
of living
more & more
like an animal,
or should I say
woman,
your eyes
pull your
voice back like

a curtain.

Near a mural
of local hero
John Dillinger's
a fire extinguisher
& Apache
scarlet snake
design blanket
I'll take my
58
cocaine black
market, our curse
to mall-dressed
Californians &
Scottsdale developers
selling
our town
off to rich brats
from Phoenix,
Los Angeles that trombonist
is hitting on
a dumbstruck
truck
driver.

Tonight,
our moon
is lit full
with piss! Cheers!

Thirty miles   away

        the families   crossing the border
ration

                their Gatorade bottles

                of water.

Tucson, 2016

San Xavier Mission, Tohono O'odham Nation

In the blue eyes of the desert
a new measure, prayer cards wet
in cathedral's shadow, a slim lizard
a dark tail, dark men I can't seem to
love in an older way. I'm describing a ghost
because I still don't understand when I was real.

I am running across the kitchen to my mother.

In the long eyes of the desert,
           I'm old enough to do without the lyrics.

Today, in the jazz of sun,
           I folded my crystal quickly,
pocket chalcedony to relieve my need for importance.

     The more I live the less I need to be someone.

     A flower or river
          are the same thing:

they empty.

South Tucson, 2018

ICE

we are
right are we
right sloppy we are
fraught we are
burdened are we
bothered we are
bastards we are
judges are we
fair we are
stoic are we
stone a quartz to wear Ivory soap
cruising Walmart retail we are
chemtrails is that
snow we are
missing children missing Legos we are
boxers we are
jeans I am
buying my friend a dildo, singing
Steve McQueen if tho we are
souls are we
souls we are
lyrical we are
authors we are
roses are we
morons we are
dancers we are
poets we were
separated from our poets
and our parents
and you put us in cages.

Tucson, 2019

Obliteration: :Moon

First time a boy   loved me back
deep-sea trench, grass fire, flammable: :sapphire animal.

The wind legs
from Louisiana where   the electrician's hand went up
a cherished   black shirt
                                    and the sky fell like a sword.

After you,   I turned the bruising in the lights slowly off.

Memory through   older, younger eyes,   a paperback on freshwater fish
suffocating in your hands   is that   my blood, he
hit me.

I carry poems,   my velvet rooms
to places   I don't escape them   in case

the Moon is handing out codes.

At the 7-11,
I'm counting out change. Cashier's scar is very bad.

Now the night   now   ghosts have,
having already wandered   from the border to streetlights: :Googled
insects

on saguaro. Horoscopes

say I have
been on fire
for so long
there is no longer
a distinction. Ablaze us,
into what   else but ash.

The witchcraft of: :our voices & sea

-shell like the Moon,   a surface forever,

they say, in light.

Tucson, 2013

Ophelia

the St. Mary's overpass,

your words getting bowled over by passing cars,

you're wearing a nylon   blue coat you had borrowed
from someone I don't know

out of cigarettes, get Pall Mall soft-packs

our world is going home, Japanese scientists
discovered a strain

of nylon-eating bacteria in a pool
of Osaka wastewater, wow that's

evolution and your coat
is at risk. You, are anyone,

driving home, overhead

hands are on steering wheels, changing

stereos, but home's not gonna be me.

What makes this world, the commute happen?
A billion years.

The moment of

a stanza's shape you recognize

it, who is it?, peer

down into words' eyes

the doll, gazing up,
but not looking back.

Orchids

Did it penetrate her eye

                                provide some last minute

investigation

                                kinesthetic flower I know

my sister ought to have been

                                fond of

your apparatus

                                bursting with emergency &

cosmic blotches

                                stargazed matrix

what strategy,

                                cancer is a strategy

restless toxicity

                                larkspurs & oleanders

venoming their beds

                                sick generosity lain

in the bloodstream did

                                you not throw a tantrum

at just the mention

                                of our father's name

the night of the road

                                side accident your mom

flung under the dark interstate

                                you saw her funeral lilacs

in waiting-room

                                lights each light,

thick, leaf desiccant

                                and irresolute, hairs

your scalp left

                                on pillow, your nod an egg-shell

buzzed-close and thinned

                                by the blare

of chemotherapy

                                in that last

bouquet having

        exhausted their own

time, Sister, dying

        in solitude you were

reading the cards in my hand

        I'm sorry

the stems

        got snagged

in my bedside manner you

        unbuttoned and held

my attention to your

        emptied breast and last words

invaded the exhaust

        of your face

my voice is hard to

        listen for

I'm waiting for

        it to provide some answer

that won't

        dig its way

out of your gravity

        the page

this poem's on

        I'm here, too

under it

        like the bone

behind

        bulge & skin

here and there

        I slept mesmerized

at your bedside, Sister,

        your passing

like the orchid I gave

        you, beginning.

Capitalism Calls Poetry Lazy

Overcast day long slack sleeves pale in February
walking through Feldman's Neighborhood
Tucson small adobe houses terra-cotta that one's prune-colored
emptied glass broken of course I move closer
pothole & smell of dog shit and barking of different
sized dogs stop. Traffic signal and cast a shadow in the bike lane.

The New York Times: Syria In Catastrophe but I see
The First World selling
its immune system
to the
same customers
it tears to pieces
I'm eating an éclair

in this café, Café Passé,   busy
with self-filled conversations:
an ex-Moron reiki master & an Orange County shaman
talk about healing movie stars online with gypsum and exercise.

I'm writing this from my disappointment, not yours.

Capitalism calls poetry lazy,

tells my poems to "go get a job." Where?
The Twin Towers?

   Economy of
      hacks, economy of shysters, but I'm loyal
to what mends me I'm in his arms in my head writing this.

I'm not economic, I want soap
and to see

a glacier,
    burdened melt light weakening
    forward from off its architecture and the snowing stops.

Allow us   to live without the States,

let us rest from voting,

let us rest   from our work, let our   hands rest

over poems, let the satellites

                fall like fruit,   let our loved ones

be buried   in earth once free,   let

rivers nomadic once roaming,   let our tools wander

in air in rain,   let our fathers

come home from prison,   let us in evening hold them

and   beneath shelter weep,

beneath shelter of   theater, beneath theater of

rising seas, let us remember

noon on a river,   our loved ones of debt,

our loved ones toiling,   still, in debt,

let our spirit of   , we forget,   spirit of plastics

spirit of optics, let spirit of rest, let us   rest from dreaming

inside your money,   so that we may

bury the ocean, let us

bury loved ones, and let us bury   the ones we've killed, let

us return the States of America, spirit of   , spirit of I forget,

Wind River, let now us   survive

our history, let us change

our names without   registration, let the ones

we've killed   be our country, may we   bury

those   we bomb,   let spirit of

                              street bums,   of the ones

we let starve, let their   begging

sit on our tongues,   once I speak,

let the ones   (drones killed my son), let us

turn our hands   to earth, to let rest

        the light be   on leaves, and let us   with names we forget

        serve who they are,   let   our

work on earth,   be forgiven,

let us be certain   we come   remorseful,

the children we've murdered,   JCPenny's

                              shirts & sheets,   let us lay

        down to leave   in our beautiful cars, in our

              medications & washing machines,   spirit of criminals, spirit of greatness,   of Earth, and spirit of   imminence,   let us

in our States, unbuild,

        and let us   once more, come home.

Office Party Yeah No Thanks

Down my office space

      whatever was ever there,

            the hours, disgusting in your families,

milk,

      but in my arms having

cubicles, the guy across from me

      his entire family died I take a shower,

            clean, a soap, a shampoo, and if I'm her, research

stupidity says beauty's symmetry,

      the distance of hand to face, I face the distance

of myself, the other side of, the boundary of

      my face makes money, an egg is .50 cents

            down the road, a guy in the Office

is professionally bettering himself, how

      Capitalism of you, Scott, his holiness, his shit paycheck

the loudest fucking wreck of my head, the clothes

      hang off my soul, it's one thing

to make yourself disappear in the symmetry of some asshole

smirking cause cocky ambivalence they've

    built gas chambers yes you can

cook an egg or three, how

tedious It is exactly a larger unit

    I descend from children I come

        to you again as kin, as ink moving like a bird

what is it inside us it sees itself

        out there, in the desert, when I look it's

underground my mouth,

    when I start talking,

        louder the quiet.

A Linguist Calls Your Shoshone Language "Data"

Considering the moon in its quarantine,
wanting to be here, with us, imagine our heads
no longer tilting up, but here, we're reading Macbeth.

                                        I think of
                    the White ghosts of Massacre Rocks, Idaho.
            Whose trail had come to a trickle in the narrows of stone.
                            I don't imagine a single person
                            turned back having come so far.
            And how they must have rode, rifle-ready, eye straining
                                    for a Shoshone.

Completive Object

I sleep
by a stranger
the night before
love is
an explanation.

You,
one,
of me,
says I
can't say that,
delighted, [predictable
loving
answer].

Lilith, Arizona

I was,

I was each time,

conventional,   I say my mouth,

the wineglass,

that's no door,   I let you go,

in the lightning,

when my heart,   closed its gift,

and the earth,   found suffering,

if living,   if it's anything,

when I look into,   the gone of love,

I was a pond,   in your hands,

looked down,   could see bottom,

where the water,   I say's fire,

black vague stones,   the bottom,

were faces,   stood in features,

heads singing,   to themselves,

to overthrow,   the vessels,

our hands wrote,   in their shallow,

on the shoreside,   was I not,

                        dissolving?

I became

innards in a jar,   open, but empty,

in your path,   the wind's,

the wind's mine,   "the woods in love are still empty,"

an empty born,   who was once,

wrong & laughing,   I

dissent,   I, lover, remember

your mouth was a hand, a hand

cannot swim,   it's holding   a stone,

in the lightning,   comes the Spring,

in the lightning,   who's guiltless?,

beside the lightning,   the darkness just seemed evil.

I burnt it,   in canyon,

gave you,   a bed,

when the canyon,   I imagine,

or what of,   whose fingers,

held back,   sharp heart,

the quiet,   itself,

desires,   who then?,

I was holding,   a knife,

would not climb,   out of myself,

wind on wing,   I can,

still eat that,   white are the stars,

when the river, I say betrayal,

lifted a canyon, lowers the

wing,   it's not sky,

the water,   no,

there are no,   songs of me,

what song,   of compassion?,

I spill,   the blades,

the river,   heads,

to fill,   the kettles,

a poet,   can't be,

a poet,   both arms,

a color,   through forehead,

blows out,   a star,

dark   are my clothes,

but you,   will listen.

Ice Water, Dry River Witches' Shoppe

I work it's mostly blue glass
sometimes it's hooked loop binding
cat hair who's looking at
tiger's eye, teacup
we're in
on the magic
of the joke. Reincarnations,
what do I say to this new one now?
You're better off gay than believing in God.

The first time I saw a ghost, I was in love
I changed a lightbulb
that morning supporting new shadows
on a day I had gotten dressed.

> *Sell the earth and on it toil,*
> *Child inside a pot to boil,*
> *Fill my glass with Iraq oil,*
> *Dance thy shoes on stolen soil.*

Electric, young YouTube insect,
"How plump,"

We're heating up the planet.
We're not even doing anything about it.
Your college kids laughing into the night.

The first time I saw a ghost
my hand pressed to car window, was during
my Initiation, she said,

> *Keep worms in your doll.*

A good laugh into white cloth.

Magic is, like reading,
like kissing, it's bryophytes dividing, gliding
sapphire kaleidoscope, yellowjackets
on a mantle, who is woman on mantle,
who is darker,   of the liars,   mask   on the mantles,
looking out from poems I'm raining on myself, on the mantle,
rain in my blood as I am from Florida, on the mantle
always stepping off.

The ritual calls for

marijuana, salt & rose, angelica,
meadowsweet, willow,
water that can
be broken, "fire" on a video,
hyssop, coccyx, lark,
lily, alder from the top
of a mountain pulled up in silence, the white cloth.

The spell says,

I suspend your burdens and locked
in my lightness believe in you
too a little longer.

Tucson, 2019

Divination

Did you know that mice dream?
Black veil over your head.
Maybe you're having a veggie burger.
Maybe I'm having a diet wine.
The mice put thoughts in your witch head.
Pull back their foreskins I unveil the Future.
Satan rolls her eyes: No such thing.
In the Future, where there were no more numbers left to count.
I am the She who allows my Red Chrysanthemum.

Since the Anita Hill trial,
none of my horoscopes
have come true. Reading your pain
because I am talented in omens.

Tucson, 2020

The Moon Reversed

Insomnia, my dog, the delta
on right paw, my fingers, splayed twigs,
cold on a bowl of vanilla ice cream
silver-dollar songs of desert,
      coyotes pressed deep into the ink.

The dog we made from them, fed & loved. Asleep by the Moon reversed.

This cedar incense is really good, hygienic
someone keeps changing me into a customer, instead look at stars
between them, the sentiments,
and between them was us,
up there, like that, can you imagine it, the community food-bank lights
and the trash styrofoam trays flapping next-door
in the loud, ugly floodlights
      moonlit gnats,
     out-numbering coyotes,
      out-numbering stars.

In the stairwell,
our voices just seemed mountainous, bounding up
the strides of steps, each tone booming up
from the olde song inside us the one that doesn't
need words, but in the earliest of my bodies I am dancing,
none of this can be conveyed in my voice, not this professional one, this
one seeking recognition, even when I have gone make-believe and you have stopped listening.

We're ever brought in to believe in it, our materialization,
not what becomes of us the carrion & the crown even when I'm

   Cellular
  colonies   dreaming
      of Witchcraft.

Today, you belong to me, so I begin the ceremony.
I make a doll, its hateful silly eyes, pour milk of lily,
you have no broken heart and there is no heaven. The sea dreamt of us, but in our cities
becoming the most evil things in the world.
A poem is a fool, police sirens in the night.
If I howl, do I have a dog in my mouth?
The steps I took, to bridge us, one after another, going back,
going back years, like dolls, I do it all the time.

If you're a wild creature, you'll be wiped out.

Queen of Cups

I'm not it's not change it.
   I'm Him, the woman
     so shit ugly
    you're dead,
    so you can have all of them.

A day at the roses, a nation
   held together with little as
    outrage & votes, some real shitty oleanders
  you got there. I go to work,
slog for better, even though I know better is wilderness.

I pledge allegiance to the dishrack,
     a fruit, a fruit

    is the desire to enter, the dishes
    keep me healthy, eat salmon off the floor, eat the student loans.

I fear there's nowhere safe here
   in this poem, this space just for you and you are
  who I've never wanted to be,
           I think of that now, in my flyblown, faggy crown.

You are breakfast on Easter.
You are the silver in the prayer.
You are the beauty I want when I say *We*.

You are the water in the infirmary.
   Poured over and over again from one yellow pitcher.
  You make the beds and tell me about the moon
 as if you were the ocean.

   Peace is in the fabric of all beings.
My hands are words I'm washing dishes.

I formed to your harmony as clearly as you are
    with mine now. I feel your presence, the injury sustained in France. You understand this
is
    where your body will be stowed. I am proud of you, but I don't want you now. Give unreal
      beings voices, say them forms alive, slabs & panels
    in the hourglass of dinner and chores, near a new Colorado burning forest.

You have nothing to lose; you have everything to lose.

    The Witch chants,

This is My body;
    a shrine You burned, so I
      am this light.

During a tarot reading, the Queen of Cups is pulled. *Enter, for I am poor and crossed,*
    and at one with my orphan. The spread your Witch has laid out for me:
      undoubtedly tragic, wise. Torn out from the future,
        devoured, passed off as folk magic.

    The heart didn't know it could die, it wasn't prepared, I look for you in faces, like a child.
Its will is authentic, can't
    steady it I was never sorry

        that I'm at peace with my evil, being gentle, the mirror you hate.

Peace is unpleasant, it's not fulfilling. You can't give it to me.

    I wouldn't recognize it, wouldn't want yours to make me stupid, the ex-military student
      from the Bay Area shows us a PowerPoint of a
        micro   waved, Middle East   city
    this country paid him to scour because
      assholes like him have
    to show us PowerPoints like this.

This Great Future
    that won't mourn us. Even now you don't. At the recycle bin
    He kissed my neck, my reusable grocery bags
      holding thighs warm as engines.

The Queen of Cups swims to shore,

enduring not her way, but hers in ours. The Queen is in pieces, and remembered in lies,
remembered for convenience, for His legalized ease
"Wouldn't you rather fuck a mask," the smirking jerk.

Your presence, your presence of center,
your presence like a ship on fire, your presence is requested.

Sure, poetry's everywhere's. When I find it in myself,
I'm scared hands in a dark room, two boats ivory at sea.
No media for the islands gone under water. I face you, and my cup is closed.

Cortez, 2021

Spell for Sedition

He wanted us
        to be dead as dead
as Him
        but I, what is everything

knows that
        a witch is
the wind talking
        what can't be

decides nothing
        and so is
immortal you
        ask what it's like

here there
        are no words for it.

With Witchcraft
        I'll escape

with teeth & page
        to a dark

sharp skull
        I am
now a stranger
        female & male,

a weapon
        of the future.

Old feathers
                    given

by a coven sister

when pressed
                    to face, to chest
            re-fly.

Wasn't I
                    your Sister
less like your
                    nun you

thought to
                    grind me
like a child
                    down into your

lessons, emulate
                    your bullshit President
I will
                    read in my voice

an emblem
                    of no one.

What

                    may fall is beautiful
broken era
                    pointed teeth
in a bizarre sandwich,

                    possesses
all of us
                    you grace

everything I have ever made.

Spell to be Said in Wind

I can
        move slowly
like a knife
        I will mend
my sedition
        and pronounce you
dead I
        don't want
to work
        for device
I wanted
        a body,
didn't we?

Now

The moil remains the compass hand
throws forward, touches sword but that
was just a thirst, fictitious I endured
your directions I would come to meet
cities, rivers, heirlooms what good is the
heart even now, earthly, made of animal
dining on empty, like a doll? You say all
of our children are naturally democratic,
well if I return to nothing, then now is
the soul.

Brian Susan

Please help me, I'm sick. Why there was no one else, what I've done.
Don't you limit me. The lot of you, impersonating revolutionists. The only real
place worth any damn was
our vengeance. And their mirrors? Big plans
to turn myself   into fierce birds. We fuck up so often, don't we?
Are you getting this, stupid?
Back there,   in the nurse's lounge no stop—change this style
because you are not alive yet, though soon, I am speaking to you now:
This is the power of our species.

I hear Susan laughing, I think it's her voice but it's just the bowl moving on its own
across the kitchen counter then into talking to the walls,
through the eyeholes in the mask upside down on her face,
I can't always tell the difference when I'm manipulating myself I'm wearing gloves
to summon them
in their masculine action
laughing now,
my fated form is? Oh, I'm being silly again.

my own pointless to own a flower
to get magical
on timber furniture perform a Divination:

7 of Cups, the Star, 9 of Wands; yarrow shall aid.

Labyrinths and labyrinths, the Future I'm microwaving the leftovers
from when Brian and I decided to Go Green
for the Future, but the Future
wants to fall apart, wants to make realer freedoms than I.

The Instructor is shapeless, demented, a vegetarian,
the lessons, my piano, raised elbows
to make sense of myself in something else than, so another form
partly human, a perfect mostly alone, years later
my hands remember the song.

"beautiful for spacious skies"

I want to burn our governments,
our prisons, our wins, our journalism.
My hands crawl through dark books.

If the Men fall into the hole, just a knife wearing clothes?
Participated in Hell even when you loved your children.
I should say this in a museum.
All of your bloodshed is false.

My forehead is being an amulet again.

The Instructor has no style and recites himself. Now there is a Woman lamenting properly.

On auburn red smoldering morning, pandemic solo
against the piano, news that you've left.

Humanity says to further terror. When I write from my poems, beauty being dead.
How to say that?

Do you sense their auras? Their portraits?
A bunch of shitty Pilgrims,
sexless, demanding fuckers.
I'm the voice who offers poetry. Choke on it.
I'm not real but also dead. More squawking.
"A felony," says the Pilgrims,

stuffing children full of ghosts, healing them in armor.

"Do you think they could die?" The ones who died and didn't graduate?
Now, I remember you.

Why are we renewed by the undoing?
Haven't I been good? In my economic pain?

Evidence of

The White Screen.

May I be

Fractal now,

across bright phones,   *Susan?*

Survives your soul?, and I
so clumsy, would have you change me?—More you.
Because what within comes forward? In the midst of all our wreckage
wasn't there another part of us? Some part of you standing out there
beside the car? Perhaps. I was

collateral, like you say, but you say *mountain Colorado slopes in October*, uninterested
in being, where it's permanent

where it
          was always

our turn I wonder   where did we get here? Where does it matter?

Bay Area Poetry Workshop

Tiburon, scorpion weed
Budweiser, Oregon
grape, corduroy jacket, whiff
of meth wait, I wanted
to say woman
over there below tarps
leaving these suburbs
KitKat wrappers, Red Bulls, razors
writing toward what?
grad school? motivating paragraphs?
I don't understand why your characters
are so financially successful
and addicted to roller-skating?

The only boy DJing
in the rink
doesn't turn
down the music
of my body.

Look at my stupid balloon animal! My voice was outlawed for centuries.
When I, even as I
the trickiest
thing to be.

She's working on a poem called "Quality Dildo,"
making it more accessible, prosey
I say it should be automatic
to enjoy yourself your
little piece
in your hands back
arched, a storm on yourself snowing on yourself and your nervous clothes.

The boys' eyes look like soap
in the light of the roller-skating rink.

Look at them all succeeding
without even trying. Literally the worst thing,
having connections. These guys on white skates
saying "your poetry

speaks

for itself."

Tucson Adult Coloring Book

Sun-shades over squash flowers, wobbly table
veneered faux-oak yellowing jalousie silverware
wrapped in white, wiped-off counter
for us a beer-can windchime's broken
open cooling window the empty letting
sun strike my green shirt, the wind

what is always wind in my poems, comes
when it moves when we move
our 9 of Swords

Resolve through sorrow, Roxy says that
sounds like a willow.

There are no gay people in children's schoolbooks.

Although, you have to admit, we're allowed the poetry.
Cause once some guy wanted to feel modern, feel edgy
and consume my pain and embarrassment, so I
was invited to speak.

Whose experience of the world gets published? A dog

begs outside for my scrambled eggs.
No, I take it black, no sugar thanks I drop the fork
in one of the first poems I ever write.

There are children in my family
who don't know that I exist cause I'm gay.
That makes straight people sad for me.
Once I was a child,
and we lived near the beach
I would bring dry food
for the stray cats and birds.

I knew they weren't real. Just easier,
to love. Anyone who goes to the ocean

can find a shell they like enough I wasn't old enough
to know it had been another living thing's.

Cloudbanks, Barrio Viejo

I've been thinking about my dad's death,
it was a February death, early & wet
lilied-faced mask of horror a disembodied
voice coming from a table over, the clouds

an opaque odor now, a distant road
holding open old opals, broken healing stones, no
one remembered to wear a simple
face their hats are full of rainclouds.

Lousy coke from Chihuahua, thunder's loud,
electro-psychological I,
                mosaic of corazón & sword on Tucson Electric Power Building.

Did I turn the oven off? Afraid to drink tapwater, ignite me, bad particle
when my father no when the river
caught fire we all shook our heads at the waterfalls
of flames diving from the rock I'm wasting your time no one
talks about what I'm interested in and neither
do I.

Death's wings
pendulum, it
worked beautifully,

Muscle relaxer mosaic,
debris, my amulet
of housekeys, light through blue plastic, apple packaging
in ocean, in my liver, the cloudbanks daydreaming,
in the pines of the Santa Catalinas.

Virga,
under our clothes.

Our clothes say, I love you. I love you more, son, the Dead say.

The Dead wander off
into things, a wind, a plate, a milk
when the Dead go unrecognized
standing in the airs & metals, the arts from where we arose
we think they no longer sound like us, broken opals blowing tones in the
black,
their voices no longer
appearing like gentle music or documents,
as if to say we have finally seen one another,
locked eyes deeply, and decided that we no longer needed leaders.

9/11, 2017

When was I, love you in a grave, some flowers
something nice to wear, these

white carnations will do from a crystal blue vase just fine.

Your reflection on   bath water, so I see
a dead lover, between

                        light & incineration, black magnetic
light,   I remember

                you in New York
now empty,
margins

        in a poem

                a generation

Americanized by terrorism. Her

death wet how   does a glass hold water there yes like that.

All the high heels   discarded in the streets,
                        so the women could run faster.

Without you, make new
                        with another you, I still miss you.
You don't exist. You're

                as real as any real living-

room, a plywood, an ottoman, a terrorist inside us a love letter,

please change this poem. I am ashamed of

                        you all for being so goddamn moral.

Deepfake

No one has been taking the proper precautions
                 and no one cares
I knelt down in
     don't care about, care about
         oh, I don't know
me down in

        on some portrait
    disgracefully, surely
        someone I
shouldn't say, coming

up dishonored, and I
am
to be
     looking on
beyond frame black
     and white, in matte
    who'd purchase
           a future: that sorrow
             a plexiglass   so patient
it was   a heart
          that dreamt   it
    beat in a ghost
   the world's careless
giving cameras

    to children the stillness
I don't like, if I
    stand
       up in my eyes?

I just wanted the room to myself.

How truly you've hurt me is the wine tonight.

some bodies throw   no shadow, who cast no light.

We are both Men now, my mother and I.
        A woman who no longer stands there,

say we no longer stand at peaceful ends,

say instead I stand there in the room, just the sunflowers
        not texting anyone back, waiting waited

for the weather to grow silent, the city
to let off its engine, and swing

wide my doors into the night.

All Soul's Procession, Year

A little girl holding chrysanthemums.
Everyone was worried about a mass shooting.

Lugging vigil boxes, hang lights, I love you
on skulls, garlands, huge cat mask, mariachi band,
improvised star on altar, Fresca soda can.

The black watercolors
                            each other
darker our bodies all of us certain

        the Dead have repaired themselves in Heaven, made themselves

young, grin

        in bed   I say they do   because the money I gave

for white chrysanthemums knows that was a long time ago

when we sent things by mail, Ben's arm
against a chinaberry tree even now,
he looks over at me holding this new one.

He circles the trunk, stands on a root to better his view,
this word for two men in love, will never exist, though the necklace

of love, herself, is

long. She says, "I'm tired

of people in love." But the money I gave

for white chrysanthemums, I throw

in a hole   a hole is still,

is something, is nothing, this place

        that kills us.

Ben,

your eyes feel good like going upstairs
to grab a pen or when I see running horses
Arizona Burger King.

You sometimes touch me like old photographs
of family I can no longer bring myself to look at.

When I read someone's fortune,
I show them how we change each other,
in this mosaic, of musical
soil & twirl, the Hanged Man
says you're still holding
on to parts
someone else
has let go.

Ben,

It takes so long to drive through Texas,
all the loud grand clouds ablaze above the midlands.

I'm turning my body in music, lifting my hands
high in night air, and a box fan cools & whirs
like wheels somewhere in a distance
that doesn't exist.

Ben,

poetry always seems bigger than me,
our best is what we'll call Art, so for now the drywall
and its doorframe with your name's initials will have to do, but tonight not the plywood
I would rather sleep, just humans under sheets.

The Texas night and the loss of our rights,
and still, the wind is in my hand, San Antonio.

Long is the highway, but all of the stars.

Interstate 10, Texas 2018

Interstate 117, the Narrows

I write perplexing rock leans in instead window,
granite gives way to pine barrens
high desert's sky's firestruck timbers
hold up a small backdrop of clouds with words.

Stranded white snow for some odd reason
on a long-pine having stolen
flowers near weird arms of a river lain
in closeness I wrote those branches down
two days from now.

I'm on a drive so I might talk about beauty.
Not love or wanting to love an object beautiful

Being left alone there
is very beautiful here I say "flower fragments"
for the first time in my life.

Burning biome poem, but not how fire called us to be created,

mossy mounds of new
blackjack pines, No I

need to speak without names to thing the world.
A path of flagstones and basalt rocks escort me back to what locals call "The Narrows,"
a longstanding Acoma trail scrambling along cliff edges.

I'm on this drive beautifully I'll hold them close to me

dust mites, mold, biomorphs

loblolly pine   needles spin asymmetrical the science
you taught me   it's the Earth who made
                      all the Living and all the Dead. The Edifice, Dirty Great Tower.

But, the white nights when our bombs fell upon Fallujah, I did a crossword puzzle
and answered
with 4 words:

    primal, national
deceased, and was *born*

      but something
I saw in the Narrows what there were no words for
say it the best I could now

[a hand raised to hush]

This poem died
when you taught me. Poetry is how I try it on.

-El Malpais Wilderness, New Mexico

Wildflower Season—Cochise County, Arizona

This is the driest
time, light harsh   a   flat sun

            scrapes lake
grieves
     a dead killer bee   pluck a mute

Mojave aster   closed open at
the day's sabotaging light.

The lonely
          of an extinct volcano,

florets of tatalencho,   hooker's evening

          primrose draw hoods
      petals up tight   left-hand

of you a cactus
wren now

rabbitfoot pocked earth
           scurry

through rainwater maybe toward
the ironwood after

that thorn miasma, teddy bear   chollas.

They stay the pen

      of poet struggling to keep
      the view of it   unhuman.

Spider Rock Canyon, 2013

Killer Queen echoing up river gorge
from a rusted black Chevy.

Roxy and I tried to reach the buckle

      in the high rock cliff face is what wind
hits coming off the rez.

The cedars early May cicadas need   on windblown bark.

        A lightning-hit pine on the northslope

      I say's got a jumpingspider on it.

Roxy is rinsing pans, tongs off

        our only spoon, her thermos
        light arcs through the waterstream,

tousled knives the cupboards,

each one discovered   behind more
particleboard,

they were spotless   ready to cut dreamy vegetables.

        "He would leave pornography out for us children to find."

Beautiful in certainty, you're a place to speak;

        I was sharp stones
        tumbling lightly against a slope.

The edge
of a showercloud pleasures us

vanishing pastel rockface.

Gunshot deer brains dry out near Spider Woman Rock.

"She has a strange mouth like Stephen King."

né'éshjaa' yilkee'é   tł'ée' íigahiits'óóz
"owl-like foot"   "white at night"
bitterweed   *white-stemmed evening primrose*

Close the book,
          "I mustn't know their names, so I won't forget."

When I'm White on the rez,   I should ask

    "Whose hands have mine belonged to?"

    "Dark hands, good enough to put diamonds on,"

                     the Presidents say.

Only there were animals in the forest where there
were no more eyes to open.

Zuni Pueblo at Shalako

We met in grad school studying linguistics,
she invited me here, desert precipice New Mexico.

"The stars aren't big just because they are so far away."

It's a privilege I write

deer-mask white

he held its long nose,
singing in like echo, raised it
to water, eyes in dark clothes.

Anywhere a mask goes

on a hill where I smell   juniper burn

drifts, intentionally   she says, where they'll run down from there.

Another dance, around midnight   transparent & red, in the glass of the dance

                                        the Mudheads motion upward.

A Coca-Cola machine,   plug buzzes in the wind.

I'm noticeable, a guest to the poetry here.
I can't

understand, the basket with a black stripe,

the technology of the basket

is just something I mention.

Whites inherited a power we killed for.

The memory to forget

children underground college campuses

The body is a long river, every one of our forms hands it to us,
Looking back at a sky in front of us.

I am tired of being haunted and without honor.
This story has been between us for centuries. Leave a space here for questions.

You don't have to know anyone to write a poem,
　　　　but you do need a language you don't really understand.

In stripes & stars? Shot up
into fireworks I applaud?

Children white, with eyes like air.

I am so tired of the headlights in the road, and all the valor you go on about.

children underground my regional bank.

Too many ghosts speaking at once.　　　We won't see it coming.

Giardia River

analyzing second-hand medicine,
velvety & hidden in the Color Purple, keep it
fire escape begin treatment, haven't I lived,
concrete wall,
convinced myself of what was in front of me,
cut myself open with what was in front of me,
kill all the detectives we invited to dinner,
weren't we supposed to, as if
we were a common people?

Old snow on dark sentences, surveillance camera lights.
I put two water jugs in the water to cool the water I had to buy.

Darks on yellows light setting, light on white dryer
silk flowers across the bike memorial,
a girl 19 studying art
bluest iris but bluer the alley you're down by
ran over, ran her over
with a moving van.

This part of us most beautiful, the part
that comes back, in strangers, in everywhere, returns
having walked from our familiar elements,
casting shadows home
birds to a drinking fountain,
on my phone
consuming emotions, it happened so long ago
that I was singular in my anger.

In Paris on the white bridge,
your eyes serve these years to me,
a light shaft on Nike's no arms,
on knights' armor, lances,
aristocrats, their wine glasses you spoke of

the dismembered Kurdish girls,
men only sorry for the ones they hadn't killed.

If the Universe curves,
scientists say it curves gently,
returning where it begins,
all of us drink it.

About the Author

Wyatt Welch grew up on the Interstates after being kidnapped by their father, a Vietnam veteran. Watching the boundaries of Self and the State has been the work of their recent poetry, alongside other poetic concerns such as living gay/transgender in the United States.

CPSIA information can be obtained
at www.ICGtesting.com
Printed in the USA
LVHW052142080523
746427LV00004B/757

9 781953 447586